Toddler Weaning:

Deciding to Gradually Wean Your Toddler & Making it Happen

Punita C. Rice, Ed.D

Dr. Punita C. Rice Ed.D

Toddler Weaning:
Deciding to Gradually Wean Your Toddler & Making it Happen
Written by Punita C. Rice, Ed.D

Originally published 2019

Selected components of this work originally appeared with the approval of the author at "Happy Mom Guide" (happymomguide.com).

More information about the author is available from PunitaRice.com
Related content is available at HappyMomGuide.com

CONTENTS

Dedicated to you, the nursing mama.

FOREWORD

This is a (short) book about weaning a breastfeeding toddler. I assume, if you are reading this book, it is because you are presently breastfeeding in some capacity, have been doing so for some time now, and are now turning your eye to bringing this chapter in your relationship with your child to a close.

This book is not a memoir, and though it contains my personal experiences, it is not really *about me*. Yet it feels relevant to share my own experience with weaning before launching into this book. I nursed my older son for less time than I would have liked, but I'm grateful for the time I did spend getting to nurse him. When weaned, I found that there were more emotions than I expected (in this book, I'll talk a little about why weaning can be hard emotionally), but I was fortunate in that the actual process turned out to not be very difficult for us. The approach we used -- a staggered approach to weaning, starting with night-weaning, and finishing with full day-time weaning -- worked for us, and that is what this book is about: an approach that worked for us.

Every mother-child breastfeeding dyad is unique, and what works for one pair in terms of sustaining -- or, as in the subject matter of this book, ending -- that breastfeeding relationship is also unique. I am not an expert on breastfeeding: I don't have a lactation consultant certification, I'm not a nurse, and I'm not even a La Leche League volunteer. I am however, a teacher and writer, and am comfortable providing detailed, written instructions. I am also a mom of two who has been lucky enough to have a positive experience with breastfeeding. And bringing a breastfeeding relationship to a close -- and doing so in a loving, sensitive way -- was also important to me. In this book, I'll share what I have learned, share my experiences, and also offer guidance rooted in my own experience. What works for me, it should go without saying, may not work for you and your family, but it may be a good place to start.

What follows is some background before we dive in.

What do we mean by breastfeeding?

Breastfeeding is feeding a baby with milk from his/her mother's breasts; this can be through pumping milk, expressing it, or feeding directly from the mother's breasts, also referred to as nursing. Breastfeeding can be done exclusively, or in combination with other forms of feeding. It can refer to giving your child the product of the breasts (milk), or to the act of nursing a child at the breast.

A note here about language: breastfeeding, in the US, is typically used to mean breast-*milk* feeding, but not necessarily feeding directly at the breast. In contrast, breastfeeding can also refer to nursing, or breastfeeding directly at a mother's breasts. In this book, I refer more to the latter definition.

As an aside, certainly, it is interesting that the term "breastfeeding" refers both to nursing at the breast, as well as bottle feeding previously pumped or expressed breastmilk; thus, the term encompasses the process (nursing at the breast) as well as the product (human breast milk) interchangeably. Though this does raise some intriguing questions about the implications for how we perceive[1] breastfeeding and nursing societally, this book, however, does not examine this distinction.

According to the World Health Organization (WHO), breastfeeding is the normal way of providing young infants with the nutrients they need for healthy growth and development.

Why breastfeed at all?

Breastfeeding is important for a baby and a toddler's health. Breast milk itself is healthy for a baby, and the production of that milk is healthy for a mother. According to WebMD, a mother's breast milk contains "antibodies that help your baby fight off viruses and bacteria" — including serious disease — and even "lowers your baby's risk of having asthma or allergies." For the nursing mother, breastfeeding lowers the risk of breast and other types of cancer and disease.

The benefits of breastfeeding are far too great in number to list here; you, as a nursing mother of a toddler, are already likely familiar with most of them. However, I'll add one of my favorite benefits here: Breastfeeding can offer pain relief. Not only can breast milk itself be analgesic, but breastfeeding (and in this context, I refer specifically to nursing at the breast itself) also has incredible value for bonding and connecting,(and, as we know, about a million other things).

Who should breastfeed?

All new mothers of newborn babies should, ideally, and if able, breastfeed their infants. Of course there are situations that might prevent this from happening, but if they have good information, and support, in theory, a great many mothers can breastfeed.

In fact, WHO suggests "virtually all mothers" are able to breastfeed (although this is not quite accurate),

...provided they have accurate information, and the support of their family, the health care system and society at

large.

Of course, this is not the full story: there are absolutely a number of circumstances that might prevent a mother from being able to breastfeed. For example, though it is not incredibly common, some women have Insufficient Glandular Tissue, which can prevent them from being able to produce enough milk for their baby (you can learn more about IGT at KellyMom.com). This is just one of many possible medical and/or physical conditions that might prevent a mother from being able to successfully breastfeed at all, or as much as she might wish. Sometimes, moms with conditions or circumstances such as these are still able to nurse, often in combination with other forms of feeding their babies.

But for most women, the lack of support from family, health care providers, and/or society in general, as WHO suggests, is the cause of the issue. That lack of support is often the source of the problem for most breastfeeding relationships that don't work out; most mothers do not have all of these supports. Some even find their health care system — i.e. hospitals — are unsupportive; many moms are given formula while in the hospital, which can function as a deterrent to breastfeeding. And this might factor into why many moms do not meet their breastfeeding "goal." However, if you are reading this book, you have likely managed to sustain a breastfeeding relationship, either because you have had these described supports, or in spite of not having them.

What about weaning?

There are many approaches to thinking about, and actually implementing, weaning. No single approach is right for everyone. And not everyone even believes that actively weaning a child from nursing is the ideal way to end a breastfeeding relationship. Moreover, the way that weaning looks will also depend on how much you are still nursing your toddler -- and like breastfeeding in the first place, this may be dependent upon a number of factors both in and out of a mom's control. The list of possible ways a nursing relationship between a mama and her toddler may look is endless; whether you've been ecologically nursing or mostly pumping, whether you're combination feeding or exclusively nursing, you could still find yourself in a position where you now need to wean a toddler.

All that said, since you are reading this book, regardless of how your nursing relationship now looks, I assume that you have not, as yet, actively fully weaned your child from the breast. Additionally, it should be noted that weaning may actually refer to the process of introducing into a child's diet anything that is not the mother's milk. That is to say, as soon as you introduced solids, you technically already started part of the weaning process. That said, in more colloquial language, we tend to use the term weaning to mean actively stopping a child from nursing at the breast. That is the topic at the core of this book, and what follows is a discussion of deciding to wean.

CHAPTER 1

Deciding to Wean

Eventually, breastfeeding comes to an end. There are a lot of camps you might fall into when it comes to weaning. In the U.S., the average mother/baby dyad has actively weaned between 3 and 6 months, though since this is a book about toddler weaning, this does not apply to you. On the other end of the spectrum are moms who extend that breastfeeding relationship past that point. If you do not buy into the self-weaning idea, and want to do something to encourage the weaning process (or rather, to discourage breastfeeding from continuing), you may be thinking about whether or not to wean, and/or whether this is the right time to do so. Ultimately, however, these are just ideas; the decision to wean has to feel right for you and your child, and your unique circumstances.

If you're not entirely certain you want to wean, it can be helpful to think through *why* you want to wean. It can be helpful to start thinking about why you want to wean, and get it down on paper. Not everyone thinks through their decision-making in the same way, but what tends to work for me when I am stuck on a decision is to make a simple, two-column chart. In the first column, I might list the reasons I am considering a particular course of action (in this case, weaning); in the second column, I might list arguments I have against each reason. As an example, I might want to wean because *I want to wear regular, non-nursing bras*. And my arguments against that reason might be *I can find more comfortable nursing bras*, and *I will eventually go back to wearing regular bras*. For me, since these "arguments against" are convincing enough that my original reason no longer holds, I would actually cross out that original reason. Thus, my desire to wear regular bras is no longer a factor in my decision making. By the end of my list-making, I can clearly see what reasons remain (are not crossed out), and can make a decision from there.

To get you started, I'm offering some possible reasons a mom might want to wean, presented as questions you might ask yourself when considering wean your toddler:

Do I want to wean because my child has reached a certain age and I feel he/she should be done?

Do I want to wean because I feel embarrassed or awkward nursing my child in public now?

Do I want to wean because of social pressure to stop nursing?

Do I want to wean because I want more sleep?

Do I want to wean because I want to get pregnant again (and breastfeeding is inhibiting my ovulation)?

All of the above reasons are valid reasons to stop nursing if that is what you want. But let us assume for a moment that you have one or more of the above concerns, but aside from that, you actually would want to continue nursing. I would suggest then, that these concerns are not necessarily reasons in and of themselves to wean; below, I'm discussing some of these issues nursing moms might have, and suggesting why they might not necessarily mean you *have* to wean -- you might still want to, but it might be worth considering why you do not have to.

"My child just turned 1 (or 2, or 3)!"

If you're a breastfeeding mother of a toddler (which I assume you are as you're reading this book), you know that it's great you've breastfed for at least[2] the first year of your child's life. First, according to the American Academy of Pediatrics (AAP), mothers should breastfeed their babies for at least one year, but ideally, longer -- and meanwhile, WHO says mothers should breastfeed their babies for at least two years, but ideally longer. Notice neither organization says that you *should* stop at 1 or 2 (or 3, or 4). Breastfeeding, instead, should continue for as long as you and/or your child decide to stop.

Beyond the first year, according to the AAP (as cited at breastfeeding resource site KellyMom), breastfeeding continues to offer "significant health and developmental benefits for the child and the mother." The AAP and the American College of Obstetricians and Gynecologists (ACOG), together in their Breastfeeding Handbook for Physicians also address the question of when moms should stop breastfeeding, and share that there's no scientific indication that there should be an "upper limit" or age for stopping breastfeeding, or at which breastfeeding becomes inappropriate or unhelpful. As to the question of whether there is an upper limit to the duration of breastfeeding: Data on the scientific foundation for "an age above which it is inappropriate or harmful to the child to continue breastfeeding" *do not exist.*

Nor are there reported risks to this method of social/nutritional interactions. Simply put, you don't *have* to stop breastfeeding because you reach some arbitrary age. When you decide to end that breastfeeding relationship is an extremely personal decision, but you should know, before proceeding with weaning, that you need not choose to wean solely because you think you have reached a time-limit on breastfeeding. A nursing relationship can continue for years -- while culturally in the Western world, this is not widely accepted or even acknowledged, it *is* a timeframe that is biologically natural and healthy, and you can extend nursing for as long as it's mutually comfortable and pleasant for you and your child. You need not wean because of a birthday.

◆ ◆ ◆

"It's embarrassing to nurse in public now."

First, know that Moms are legally allowed to breastfeed wherever they want (that is to say, anywhere the mom is legally allowed to be). Breastfeeding in public is perfectly legal in all 50 states now. That said, nursing an older baby or toddler might feel odd[3] for some moms. This isn't a book meant to pass judgment on the politics of nursing your older toddler in public, and moms who are comfortable doing so, *keep fighting the good fight!* But many moms feel less comfortable or confident nursing an older child in public, and many others may even find it to be a logistical nightmare: your 18 month old who can't sit still just might not be as cooperative nursing privately in your lap at a restaurant as he would have at 2 months.

Instead of weaning entirely, maybe you'll be happier simply restricting nursing to certain times or locations. Think back to the beginning, as you were trying to become comfortable with breastfeeding: you might have preferred to breastfeed where you were most comfortable -- at home, in bed, on a favorite chair -- you might find it easier and more peaceful to revert to breastfeeding *only* in those kinds of places. You might also find it helpful to implement *some* of the "how-tos" in this book to limit the number of times you nurse in a day, rather than to wean entirely.

◆ ◆ ◆

"I feel pressure to stop nursing."

If you want to take a stand against people in your life who might be pressuring you to stop breastfeeding, know that science is on your side. You can certainly be the one to educate the naysayers in your life (who are most likely expressing their disapproval out of genuine ignorance). If you want to educate the people who come at you with negative feedback or pressure about your continued breastfeeding relationship, you can offer them facts: Breastfeeding past 12 months still offers the same benefits as before; breastmilk continues to benefit the baby, and nursing still benefits mom; etc. You can also combat rude remarks with humor, or acknowledge the person's opinion (and then just do you). You can also choose to approach this in the same way as you might approach feeling awkward about nursing in public: just don't do it around the people who are pressuring you.

That said, pressure is not inherently bad; it may be worth stopping to consider *why* you are being pressured to stop. Everyone's situation is different. Perhaps you're being pressured to stop by an OB/GYN who feels strongly that it would be unwise for you to continue to breastfeed through a high-risk pregnancy; in that case, it might be wiser to take the pressure a bit more seriously. Perhaps you're being pressured by your partner to stop breastfeeding because you've not yet started ovulating and the two of you would both like to conceive another baby. But if you're being pressured to stop breastfeeding by people who really shouldn't get a say in your breastfeeding relationship (that is: everyone other than, perhaps, your partner, and your healthcare provider), you can probably safely tune them out. And it can be helpful to consider that sometimes, others' comments are simply rooted in their own philosophies and beliefs that differ from yours -- thus, they need not influence you. And often, negative comments and pressure are rooted in ignorance (or maybe judgment or even disgust), and in those cases, you definitely do not need to let them influence you. The wisest course of action is to do what you want -- not necessarily to wean as a response to it.

"I want to get pregnant (and breastfeeding is inhibiting ovulation)."

Many mothers who breastfeed, even moms who breastfeed exclusively, experience a return of fertility after a few short months (and get their periods and ovulation back early on) -- but many others do not. In some cases it's because they're following the principles of ecological breastfeeding (which I'll discuss shortly), but in other cases, it can just be down to the mom's individual body chemistry and hormonal balance. Breastfeeding (and attachment parenting) advocate Dr. Sears explains that breastfeeding can end up serving as a form of birth control (as does La Leche League).

If you've heard a hundred times "you can get pregnant while breastfeeding, even exclusively breastfeeding," and think you can be fertile while pregnant, you're definitely not wrong. But it doesn't always work out that way, and there is something you can do that can help prevent a pregnancy while nursing: practicing ecological breastfeeding.

Your likelihood of not being fertile while breastfeeding is higher (or, phrased differently, your fertility is lower) if you're practicing something called ecological breastfeeding — which means you're really not as likely to get pregnant. Ecological Breastfeeding is something different from Exclusive Breastfeeding; ecological breastfeeding means following the "seven standards of ecological breastfeeding" (from the book *The Seven Standards of Ecological Breastfeeding: The Frequency Factor* by Sheila Kippley):

1. Breastfeed exclusively for the first six months (not even water)
2. Comfort baby at your breasts
3. Avoid bottles and pacifiers
4. Sleep with baby for night feedings
5. Nap with baby for nap feedings
6. Nurse frequently day and night, avoiding schedules
7. Avoid any practice that restricts nursing or separates you from baby.

According to ModernAlternativeMama.com, there is a "difference between ecological [breastfeeding] and exclusive breastfeeding... ecological breastfeeding is a viable option for natural child spacing [if] following the Seven Standards [of Ecological Breastfeeding]."

It's easy to see how the "rules" can be super restrictive -- or even impossible -- for most moms in the modern world (even more so for moms who work outside the home/away from baby!).

However, it is possible that you, the reader of this book, *do* adhere to many, or maybe nearly all, of these standards. And for moms who do adhere to these standards, and especially for those who continue to do so well past the first year, there is the chance that your breastfeeding relationship is preventing pregnancy. Moms who stick to these standards typically don't experience a return to fertility until after they stop adhering to some of those standards; if they continue following them, they don't typically see a return to fertility until at least after the one year mark.

In fact, according to a 1999 study from Jen O'Quinn on natural child spacing and breastfeeding, close to half (48%) see a return to fertility when their baby is somewhere between 12 months and 24 months old. The chart that follows shows the findings[4] from the Jen O'Quinn study.

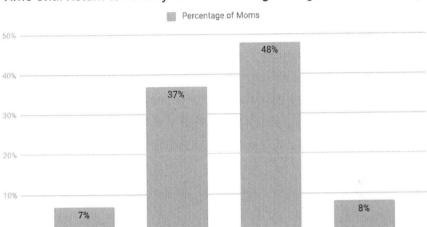

Time Until Return to Fertility While Practicing Ecological Breastfeeding

As an aside, this is actually considered an advantage to many moms, and is also referred to as Natural Child Spacing. Basically, the idea is that if moms practice true "ecological breastfeeding," it will inhibit fertility, which can be a great and convenient thing (unless you want to get pregnant again). All this makes sense intuitively, too; if you're following these "rules," it's almost like you're communicating to your body, "I'm already busy nourishing a baby around the clock; don't make another one yet please."

As someone who did not want to get pregnant until my older son was at least 1, I assumed I'd have to be very careful to avoid pregnancy. But when my nursing toddler was 12 months old... and then 13 months... and then 14 months, and neither my period or any signs of ovulation were anywhere in sight, I started to consider that maybe it was something I was doing that was inhibiting my fertility. And of course, that was exactly right, because I had been following the standards of ecological breastfeeding: breastfeeding on demand, comforting at the breast, avoiding any fake nipples (pacis, binkies, dummies), co-sleeping, co-napping, nursing on demand, and sticking to my baby like glue (lots of babywearing and rarely being away from him). And all of these were, of course, tied to ecological breastfeeding, and therefore associated with inhibiting pregnancy. In my case, adherence to the standards of ecological breastfeeding were absolutely factors in why I wasn't fertile yet, and therefore, why I was not getting pregnant. Obviously, what worked for my body might not work for someone else's body, but in my case, once I fully weaned, I was able to experience an immediate return to fertility. Thus, if you want to get pregnant again, and you're still nursing, and you haven't yet ovulated, it's *possible* that weaning might be the thing that makes you ovulate.

By the way, it might also be that "cutting back" on nursing does the trick; some moms find day-weaning or night-weaning does the trick. I personally wanted to get pregnant without having to wean first, and was hoping that just cutting back on nursing, by night-weaning[5] (as discussed in the next section), would be enough of a shift away from ecological breastfeeding that it would bring back fertility. It didn't work for me, and I ended up having to fully wean to get pregnant, but of course, your mileage may vary. Toddler weaning may not mean an instant return to fertility for everyone. Everyone will have a completely different experience, and everyone's body is different, and fertility and conception are complicated. But based solely on my own experience, weaning my toddler did mean a return to fertility. We fully weaned when my son was 18 months old, and about a month later, my fertility did return. Knowing what I know now, I don't wish I had proceeded any differently; I realize now that if I had weaned sooner, I might have been able to conceive another baby sooner; but I also would have ended my nursing relationship with my older child at a time that wasn't right.

On the other hand, this might not at all be your issue. Most moms are not necessarily unable to get pregnant while nursing;

put less confusingly: breastfeeding does not function as birth control for most mothers. This is partly because, for the most part, most nursing mothers are not following the standards of something called "ecological breastfeeding" (discussed in a moment). We all know moms who end up pregnant, whether intentionally or not, within the first year of having a baby, even if they were still nursing. And we know also likely all know moms who have nursed well past a year but got their periods/ovulation back far sooner than the point at which they weaned. And indeed, there also those moms who nurse through a second or subsequent pregnancy, and even go on to tandem nurse. If you're a mom who is still nursing, and you're ovulating and/or looking at a second pregnancy, you obviously know that for many women, it is possible to become pregnant while nursing! It may be that for you, you just want to wean because you want to get pregnant (or are pregnant), but simply do not want to be nursing through a pregnancy. In this case, you might well decide to wean.

Alternatively, you might be interested in nursing through a pregnancy, which is an option for some women (again, it depends on your body and your individual health circumstances; this is something to discuss with your healthcare provider). Some moms also want to tandem nurse following another pregnancy. These might be a feasible ideas for you, and you might end up deciding *not* to wean for this reason.

"I want more sleep at night."

Possibly, if you're finding that your sleep is often disturbed by the nursing needs of your toddler, you are considering weaning in order to maximize your sleep. First, it has to be stated that weaning, whether entirely or only at night, is not going to eliminate night *parenting*. You'll still have to wake up at night to attend to your child's various needs. That said, *if* you are truly suffering sleep deprivation and you are certain that continuing to nurse your toddler at night is the actual cause -- you might be considering weaning. Rather than fully weaning, however, you might consider co-sleeping with your toddler to make nursing easier, or *only* night-weaning (and continuing to nurse during the waking hours).

Of course, co-sleeping with a toddler is not perfect for everyone (and the pros and cons of doing so are not really the focus of this book), but *can* be a solution for some moms who want to continue nursing but would prefer not to get out of bed and ruin their sleep. Additionally, assuming you're still planning to wean in the somewhat near future, co-sleeping (if you're not already doing so) is not really a step in that direction.

Night-weaning, then, might be a solution for moms who are nursing toddlers around the clock, and want to limit it a little. For us, night nursing and bed-sharing were convenient, and I found it convenient to be able to meet my child's needs and have us both quickly drift back to sleep. But some time early in the second year, I started to get greedy and want a night without having to even do that. Of course, as mentioned previously, night-weaning as a means of reducing night-waking is not foolproof; your child, like mine did, will still have needs some nights that will require you to wake up, perhaps even to wake up far more than you were used to having to do to nurse. But if you've been nursing at night for the past year or more, and you're starting to crave uninterrupted sleep, it is possible that night-weaning will do that for you. Later in this book, I offer an overview of how we night weaned.

"I'm just ready to be done."

It may well be that you are simply *over it*, and that is fine. However, it may well be that you would like to continue nursing, but these are the things motivating you to stop, and these are, in fact, not necessarily reasons to stop if you don't really want to. Each of the above reasons is valid, and the decision to wean is entirely yours (and perhaps, your child's). If you're done, you're done.

CHAPTER 2

Why Weaning Can Be Hard

I t is also important to note that weaning can possibly be hard on your child emotionally (and certainly physically if you're weaning before they're developmentally ready), but -- and this is talked about less often, I think -- weaning can also be *hard for moms*. Many moms may have a hard time with bringing a nursing relationship to an end. This can be especially true if breastfeeding was overall a positive experience.

Weaning can be difficult because of its physical components (engorgement is not a joke), and therefore, can be difficult even if you are not still nursing at the breast. And the physiological stuff can be really hard; many moms even go through lows that are similar to depression. Part of the reasoning can be tied to the shift in hormones that accompanies weaning; as you wean, prolactin levels decrease, and you have fewer bursts of oxytocin. And of course, it can also be incredibly hard mentally and emotionally.

When I weaned my older child, I was surprised at how emotional I felt (especially the first morning my son didn't ask to nurse). Even while I'm aware of how fortunate I have been, and thankful I've been able to enjoy nursing my child, and grateful that I was able to nurse him for 18 months, bringing this part of our relationship to an end was not without difficulty. I struggled with two things, primarily: first, I felt guilt about "taking away" something from my child that was only beneficial for him, and second, I felt sad about the end of that part of our relationship.

I felt guilt about denying him a comfort that he had grown to accustomed to, even while I knew that for a variety of reasons, it was ultimately the right thing for our family at that time. For me, that guilt was assuaged by the relative ease with which my son took to night-weaning. And the intellectual awareness that weaning meant the ending of a physical oneness with my son was also hard. Of course, this was balanced by my joy at my son's growing independence, but I still found myself feeling a sense of loss. I will say, though, that my negative feelings dissipated pretty quickly after he was fully weaned.

Other mothers might have different challenges with weaning. For many families, starting the process of weaning can throw a kink into an otherwise smooth family routine. And, weaning can be especially difficult if one member of the nursing dyad is ready, while the other isn't. Still other moms have a response to weaning that ranges from celebration of their children's increasing independence (and sometimes, their own independence!) to struggling with the end of the nursing relationship with their child. Moms weaning their babies may also struggle with wondering if they're doing the right thing. (Plus, for so many moms, getting into the swing of breastfeeding can be such a complex challenge — this can make weaning even harder.) Below, I am sharing what some other mothers found to be the hardest thing about weaning.

The Hardest Thing

About Weaning

For a family that has a routine down, weaning can be a disruption. This can be especially true if your family has settled into an otherwise smooth sleep routine. Nursing moms (especially, but not exclusively, nursing moms who co-sleep) can benefit from being able to easily nurse babies to sleep or back to sleep. For my friend Cherie, who has nursed two babies for over 14 months each, giving up nursing to sleep has thus been challenging for their family:

> *"Weaning is a milestone, and definitely can be emotional as momma (and baby) may feel a little loss of closeness (and in our case, sleep). For me, the hardest part of weaning both babes has been managing sleep. We're not awesome sleep trainers, so losing my powers as the human pacifier is/ has been a significant obstacle. After over 14 months both times, it's a hard habit to break – especially in desperation at 3 am!"*

Sometimes, weaning can be difficult for a really simple reason: you're ready to stop, and your child doesn't seem ready to give it up. Says my sister-in-law Kelli:

> *"The hardest thing about weaning is that I am ready and he is not."*

...And when you feel any kind of pressure to continue, that sense of feeling ready to stop can be difficult to deal with. In her video on how to night-wean a toddler, YouTuber Amanda Muse touches on this, and says that when Mama is ready to stop nursing, that can signal that it's "right" time to end a nursing relationship. As she puts it, while the attachment parenting movement encourages mamas to breastfeed your child until the child is "ready" to stop,

> *"The whole thing is: I'm ready to stop... and it's a relationship; it's two people: it's the mommy, and it's the baby. And it stops working for either partner, then you need to come up with a solution..."*

...That solution can sometimes be weaning. Still, it can be hard to know if or when it's the right time to wean. My friend Liza, who nursed her two sons for close to two years each, shared that the hardest thing about weaning for her was struggling with not knowing if she was doing the right thing. Here's Liza:

> *"I specifically remember weaning [my older son], and holding him while he was crying thinking to myself, What am I doing? Is this right? Is this normal? We worked so hard to finally click in this breastfeeding journey and now I am saying no more, pump the breaks, sorry but that's a wrap. The feeling of guilt, sadness and helplessness taking over just like it did in the beginning when I questioned if breastfeeding was actually going to work."*

And in addition to struggling with those feelings of uncertainty, bringing the nursing relationship to an end can also make you very aware of how much, and how quickly, your baby is growing up. While that's obviously a wonderful and joyous thing, it can also be hard in the beginning. As my eloquent friend Alexandra put it:

> "The hardest thing about weaning for me was that it forced me to accept the passage of time in [my son's] life. I'm so proud of his increasing independence, but the distance always feels heavy. First he grew in my body, then he nourished through my body, and when he weaned we were only physiologically connected in that he is my heart."

I know that while I initially felt a slight sense of loss after we weaned, it was quickly replaced by admiration for my son's independence. And the truth is, weaning doesn't indicate the end of a bond between us at all. To quote Amanda Muse's video,

> "It's not always a sad story when one is ending their breastfeeding relationship, and you don't always need to feel sad about it; sometimes, it's just done. And everyday you spent breastfeeding is amazing, and you've done a great job, so pat yourself on the back."

While weaning does mark the end of one part of the mother-child relationship, it also signals the beginning of a new chapter in your child's life, and your relationship with him or her.

Why We Weaned

As mentioned previously, I wanted to wean because I wanted to get pregnant, and nursing was, for me, preventing ovulation and therefore pregnancy. Around the time that my toddler was 16 months old, I went forward with night-weaning, in hopes that it would be enough to jump-start my fertility. (It wasn't.) For the purposes of getting more sleep at night, it was nice -- though there were nights where I still had to wake up, both my son and I were finally sleeping through the night, essentially for the first time ever. But I also realized I still wasn't seeing or experiencing any signs that my fertility was returning, even after a few weeks. I realized I would have to take things up a notch.

So we made the decision to start the process of fully weaning, which happened at 18 months. As I mentioned previously, I had mixed feelings about weaning. In some ways, it was actually a little bit hard emotionally. It wasn't just because nursing made me feel like a superhero (though it kind of did) and I feared I'd miss that feeling. The thought of this chapter in my relationship with my son coming to a close made my heart ache, because it meant the end of a physical oneness between us. In the months and weeks leading up to fully weaning my son, I could relate completely to the way that writer and preacher Sarah Bessey put it:

"When I think about not breastfeeding – one of the most real things I've ever done with this body – ever again, I catch my breath with longing."

Even after weaning, I knew there would be physical closeness, and of course my son wouldn't outgrow me or whatever (not for another decade and a half maybe), but fully weaning still made me sad to think about; it still meant the end of something; I carried him inside me for 9 months, and then nourished him from my own physical being for another year and a half.

I also felt bad weaning because my son had been doing so well with our nursing relationship, and I had imagined our nursing relationship lasting a lot longer. In fact, I had really built up a (now hilarious) fantasy in my mind of how our nursing relationship would go: I thought I'd be able to continue nursing, and because I had night weaned, I hoped I'd immediately get pregnant, but that I'd continue to have a magical nursing relationship with my son, and then maybe even go on to tandem nurse, and my son and his future baby sibling would have this magical special bond because they tandem nursed and their magical mama made it all happen. Amazing. (Of course, after becoming pregnant, I was *extremely* thankful that I was not still nursing, because it would *not* have worked for me.)

For what it's worth, within a week or so after we weaned, I no longer felt any of those heavy or negative feelings. And now, months later, a pragmatic part of me understands why I felt the way I did, but also feels it was for nothing, because my bond with my son is stronger than ever, and it was nothing to worry about. (I hope and imagine that the next time around, I'll better know -- at least intellectually -- what to expect; but I will likely still wrestle with those feelings to some degree).

All things considered, I don't have regrets about when, or about how I weaned my son, and I'm grateful that for me, weaning my toddler resulted in my return to fertility. However — and not that it was always easy — I also know that I truly cherished the time I got to spend nursing my son, and I'm so thankful for that nursing experience and relationship. In the end, even though weaning was hard (for me probably as much as it was for my child), it happened. The next chapter offers an explanation for why we weaned gradually.

CHAPTER 3

The Case for Gradual Weaning

Some mothers find that weaning is extremely simple and quick, and perhaps even easy. Other mothers find the process to be miserable and long, and perhaps even anxiety-inducing. I personally was terrified about starting, and therefore decided to combat that fear by taking it slowly. For us, the entire process of gradually required a lot of on-going, active effort, but that approach actually allowed us to take our time, and therefore put me more at ease. Everyone's experience is different, but following a slow, gradual approach was perfect for us.

Going from getting my son night weaned to fully weaned took about two months, because we moved very slowly through it. I know a lot of moms quit nursing cold turkey, but I didn't want to rush the full weaning process for him, or for myself.

The slow, gradual approach can be good for mothers even if they are not nursing directly at the breast. This is to say, even if you are still providing breastmilk for your child through other means (expressing or pumping and providing your child milk with a bottle or cup), you might still benefit from taking your time with stopping. Weaning can still be challenging for you and your child, for many, if not all, of the reasons described earlier, so taking your time with weaning may still be ideal. For me, and I imagine for many moms reading these pages, taking it slow can help with the logistics of stopping the breastfeeding relationship, can give you (and your child) time to adjust mentally and emotionally, and can ease physical discomfort.

I myself wanted to go through the weaning process slowly for myself — for my own emotional mental and adjustment, as discussed in the previous chapter, and moreso, for logical, physical reasons. And, of course, for my son's sake.

First, I wanted to take my time with weaning to prevent physical discomfort and distress; during our nursing relationship, I had a bout of mastitis (mastitis is no joke — if you've ever had it, or know a nursing mom who has had it, you know just one experience with it is more than enough) once before, and also dealt with plugged ducts multiple times, so I wanted to do whatever I could to prevent those things. I knew working through fully weaning very gradually would be my best defense.

Second, but as importantly, I wanted to take our time for my son's sake. My son was happy nursing, and was thriving. And because I had already night weaned him, I didn't want to shake things up for him so much so fast. So we moved through fully weaning very slowly. Taking it slow also gave everyone time to adjust to the idea, and find new ways to comfort our son as we took away our magic wand (nursing) that had solved every single problem in the past. It also gave us time to talk it up, and get our son used to the idea long before we started making changes.

In the end, we settled on an approach that stretched out over multiple months, and involved a lot of talking and reading, and then eventually, a 3-day night weaning process, and then 8 weeks to be completely weaned.

You may decide you want to take a less gradual approach to weaning than we did. The concepts in this book can certainly be modified to your preferences. We prepared for our night-weaning weekend over the course of almost two months, but you know your child best; if you can prepare him or her for night-weaning in less time, go for it.

Similarly, we stretched the process of fully weaning over almost 8 weeks; that same approach can be modified to 6 weeks (I present an outline for this at the start of Chapter 5), but can also certainly be condensed into even less time. Simply use the guidelines for each week to fit a day or two rather than a complete week.

In the next two chapters, I will explain exactly how we night weaned, and then how we fully weaned after that.

CHAPTER 4

How to Night Wean

A s previously mentioned, in our journey to fully wean, we started with night weaning. Everyone's experience with night weaning will differ; one of my dear friends, for instance, tried to follow the process we used, and had zero luck. As with all things child-rearing related, your mileage may vary, everyone is different, and so on. That said, as I was gearing up to start night weaning, I found it really helpful to read other moms' stories and tips, and it is in that spirit that I even put this book together, and that I am sharing what worked for us.

How I Night Weaned my
Toddler 3-ish Days

The "-ish" is because really, it took over a month of preparing our son for night weaning before we actually started night weaning. And actually, then, when we finally actually night weaned, it really only took one real night of actively night weaning.

First, the background information: We started night weaning my older son when he was about sixteen months old, but started preparing him for it (by talking and reading about it) about two months earlier. Until that point, he was nursing pretty much on demand, day and night. We co-slept, and my son was still at the all-night diner every night, so to speak. Then we began.

One Month Out

About a month before night weaning, around when my son was fourteen and a half months old, I heard about, and subsequently ordered, a picture book called *Nursies When The Sun Shines*, which is meant to teach your child that from now on, they can only nurse when the sun shines. We read that book every day, multiple times a day (though we use the term *dudhu* (a toddlerized version of the Hindi and Punjabi words for milk) for milk in our house, so I substituted that for the word "nursies" whenever we read the book). We also made it a point to talk a lot about the differences between night and day, and make a big deal about how at night it was dark and Mr. Sun was gone, and that in the morning, Mr. Sun would come up.

By the way, if you're not into the idea of buying another book about night weaning, it may still be helpful to continually talk about the differences between night and day as you lead up to night weaning. But for what it's worth, if you're on the fence on buying a book specifically to prepare for night weaning: The book has beautiful illustrations, and I love that it's unclear if the child in the book is a girl or a boy. Also, the last page of the book also includes great practical tips for night weaning, including emphasizing the difference between night and day. However, it also might not work[6] for everyone.

I think that our consistency in reading this book together, and perhaps more importantly, using consistent language, was a huge helping factor in why we were able to ultimately night wean quickly. It helped us in coming up with language around not nursing at night (and only nursing during the day), and got him used to thinking about it. By the time the actual day(s) of starting night weaning came, it was easy to refer back to the language from the book, and feel confident that my son knew what I was talking about.

By the way -- if you do not feel you can devote a month to preparing your child for night weaning, devote as much time to it as you feel is realistic.

◆ ◆ ◆

One Week Out

For the week leading up to the big night-weaning weekend -- and we chose to start the process over a long weekend -- we made a huge deal about the whole *Mr. Sun comes up in the morning* thing, and also talked a lot about how soon, *you'll only have dudhu when the sun shines!* – we phrased it a lot of different ways, and talked about it excessively. We did not change anything else about his or our bedtime routine; we continued to co-sleep, and I continued to nurse on demand through the day and night. However, every chance we got, we talked to him non-stop about how things were going to change soon.

To support this, we also took a trip to Target to buy a special new sippy cup for night time. We made a big fuss about how from now on, he could have a sippy cup at night time.

During this week, my husband and I also talked a lot about how we wanted to handle the crying that would inevitably occur in this process, and whether or not we wanted to change how we handled "night parenting." Until this point, for the most part, I had always tended to our son's nighttime needs. With the exception of middle-of-the-night diapering when he was a newborn, I comforted or nursed our son whenever he woke or needed anything until this point. Some families, when starting night weaning, decide that going forward, the non-nursing parent will take over nighttime comforting. However, I felt like handing him off to Dada would be more frustrating for him, since he was so used to having me comfort him at night.

Thus, after a lot of thought, I decided that I still wanted my husband to wake up when our son and I were up, but only to provide me moral support (i.e. provide some empathy when it was tough; hold our son if I needed a break; cheer me on in our victories -- don't underestimate how valuable and affirming this can be while on this journey!). I communicated this clearly to him, and he was able to support me in exactly the way that was most helpful.

Others might find it easier or better to actually hand their child off to the non-nursing parent; this is simply what worked for us.

Regardless of what approach to night-parenting other families take during the night-weaning process, I would highly recommend communicating with your partner about everyone's roles. I am grateful I took the time to decide this ahead of time, so that there was no confusion on the night of.

Night 1: Bedtime

Then, on the actual day we were going to start night weaning my toddler, we brought his new sippy cup upstairs, filled with water, and we talked non-stop about how at night, *Mama will sleep, Dada will sleep, and dudhu will sleep at night!* For what it's worth, even though I don't think that at this age (my son was about 16 months old at this point), he had a strong understanding of "today," I really I felt like I could see a glimmer of understanding in his eyes.

Then the actual night came. That night I wore a crew-neck t-shirt to bed instead of a v-neck or loose button-down (this is to say, I wore something that would physically limit access to nursing). We talked about how there would be no milk at night, and then got in bed. I let him take a sip of water from his new sippy cup, and then tucked him in with us. We read a bedtime story, and then, it all began.

I tried, unsuccessfully, to get him to sleep without nursing. It was, admittedly, terrible (but took less time than I anticipated). It took about an hour of holding him, while he was crying for me to nurse him, until he finally fell asleep. After that was done, I was so relieved -- but I was also bracing myself, because I knew he would wake up to nurse in just a couple hours.

Night 1: The First Wake-Up

The first wake-up was probably the toughest of the night, and maybe even of the whole process. He woke up at around midnight, and I tried to pat him back to sleep and remind him that dudhu is sleeping, but he was not having any of it. He started signing for milk repeatedly. Then, when he realized I wasn't going to nurse him back to sleep, he got angry, and sad, and cried a lot, while I tried to comfort him with back rubs and cuddles. The crying and sadness continued for more than an hour.

At the same time, I was in need of a bathroom break, and was also starting to struggle with a need to express milk, I handed our son off to my husband for a few minutes. After I came back, I continued with trying to comfort him to sleep (without nursing) -- and then he started getting hysterical. I even repeatedly tried to offer him his sippy cup, and he threw it angrily.

Then, I pulled out my phone, and put on a YouTube video of mice running around and doing tricks (I searched for "mouse tricks"), and showed him the videos that came up. Weirdly, this calmed him down. Then, I offered him his sippy cup of water, and while distracted by the video, he drank from it. We cuddled in bed and watched mouse videos for maybe twenty minutes, and then he started to look drowsy. And then, like magic, while still loosely holding the sippy cup, and sitting partially propped up by my pillow, he fell asleep. At this point it was probably around 1:30am; I went back to sleep too, bracing myself for round 2.

◆ ◆ ◆

Night 1: The Second Wake-Up

The next time he woke up was around 4am. Once again, he asked to nurse, and I had to say no. But this time, I went straight to the mouse videos and sippy cup combo, and it worked. About twenty minutes later he was back asleep.

◆ ◆ ◆

Night 1: The Third Wake-Up

The next time he woke up it was, thankfully, about 6:30 in the morning, and *the sun was up*. So I cracked open the blinds slightly, and made a big fuss about how *Mr. Sun was up now*, and that means *dudhu is awake*, and he can nurse now! He was less visibly excited about it than I thought he'd be, but he nursed, and then fell back asleep for another hour. And that's it. Night 1 was complete.

◆ ◆ ◆

Nights 2 and 3: Bedtime

Getting him to fall asleep on Nights 2 and 3 took a very long time. I ended up showing him a mouse video and then hugging him and patting him to sleep both nights, and while it worked, it was exhausting.

◆ ◆ ◆

Nights 2 and 3: Wake-Ups

Both nights, he woke up 3-4 times both nights, but for the

wake ups, instead of mouse videos and water, I patted him, or rubbed his back to lull him back to sleep, and it worked!

◆ ◆ ◆

Success!

Overall, night weaning my toddler went more smoothly than I expected. I kept expecting another miserable night over the next few days and weeks, but it never came. We still continued to talk a lot about how dudhu sleeps at night, and continued reading the book. We also stayed consistent, and eventually I think he sort of just decided that waking up for water and videos of mice was not really worth it.

Tips for Night Weaning Your Toddler

Here, I have some tips based on what worked for us: (1) talk a lot about night weaning, (2) have distractions (sippy cup; videos)(3) communicate your needs to your partner, (4) take care of your own body while weaning, and (5) make sure you are truly ready and stay the course.

First, talk about night weaning (a lot!). Talking a lot about night vs. day is helpful (daytime vs. nighttime), so that when you start talking about how you'll only be nursing them during the day, they get what you mean.

Second, have distractions available. Be prepared with something that will "replace" nighttime nursing, like a sippy cup of water. Some moms prefer a cup of milk (whether expressed, or otherwise), but since I wanted everyone to get to sleeping all night, I wanted to make night wakings less tempting; I figured water would be less exciting than milk. And for when things got really out of hand, I had my phone available to offer something that could calm him down when he was getting really angry. For us, mouse videos did the trick, because they did not have too much noise or color, and were not too stimulating, but were still interesting.

Third, make it clear to your partner how they can support you. Many nursing moms have their partners take over night time comforting. This can be great for your baby, because it communicates clearly that now, the other parent (who does not or cannot nurse anyway) is now the go-to-parent at night. In my case, since I had decided this wasn't the approach we were going to take in our family, I wanted to make sure my partner knew how he could best support me. So I let him know that having him available for moral and emotional support; as I previously mentioned, I can't overstate how supportive words of affirmation/admiration can be after you manage to get your toddler to sleep without nursing, or even logistical support. And, as I previously mentioned, there was a point one night during Night 1 when I had my partner take over with our awake-and-angry son so I could hand-express to relieve engorgement, which was very helpful. And on that note...

Be careful with your breasts. Engorgement is uncomfortable. It's probably wise to be mindful of it, and to hand express a little, especially the first few nights. If you're at the point in a nursing relationship that you're night weaning a toddler, you've likely been nursing at night for a long time. That means your body has been used to producing a lot of milk at night for a long time. So be kind to your body!

Finally, I would advise nursing moms to *not* night wean until you are really ready. Just like nursing your toddler is something you yourself have to feel strongly about for the nursing relationship to work well, weaning your toddler is also something you have to feel ready for. You have to stay committed. Tat first night, there were moments that were a little heartbreaking for everyone; if I had not been committed, it would have been too easy to cave in and just nurse. Do not start the process of night weaning until or unless you're ready to do so, because it will be much harder to stay committed if you're not really ready. Thus, my best advice is that once you have determined you and your baby are ready to night wean (and you really have to be sure -- see Chapter 1), and you've decided to put your plan into action, you have to stay the course and stay committed. If you waffle or change your mind halfway through the process, it obviously will not work. And yes, there may be tears from you, too.

All things considered, night weaning my toddler was not, overall, as bad as I thought it might be. I should also mention that before we night weaned, he was also nursing during naps, so I would always be really close by. But after we night weaned, a nice bonus was that he sort of just stopped expecting to be nursed during naps as well (sleep time means no nursing, I guess). So essentially, when he was night weaned, he was also "sleep weaned."

After night weaning, we ended up fully weaning about two months later, and I started the process of "fully" weaning immediately after he was night weaned. It took the entirety of that two month period to get to fully weaned. The next chapter outlines how we got to that point.

CHAPTER 5

How to Wean a Toddler in 6-8 Weeks

As a reminder, we started the full-weaning process with our son already night weaned (at 16 months old). Then, we gradually weaned over the next couple of months. I ended up fully weaning my older son at 18 months. Now I think it's important to mention that 18 months could be perceived as early or late, depending on who you are. I'm going to pause here to address that. 18 months, for me, ended up being the right amount of time for that breastfeeding relationship.

Admittedly, if I had breastfed for longer, I imagine I would still have felt that way -- that it was the right length of time. I think it's important to acknowledge that what constitutes the right amount of time to devote to a nursing relationship (or not enough time, or even too much time) varies from mother to mother. I also recognize that my son's age at the time of weaning played a large part in the successes (and challenges) we had in weaning. Another mother, weaning her child from the breast at a different age, is likely to have a different experience. To be fair, though, another mother is likely to face different challenges and successes anyway, because she is a different person from me, and her nursing child is a different one from my own -- but I have no digressed more than I intended. To bring things back, I'll share the plan I used to wean. Here's Weaning a Toddler in 6 Weeks:

Weaning a Toddler in 6 Weeks:

Week 1 – Don't offer, don't refuse

Week 2 – Get down to a manageable 4 nursings a day

Week 3 – Get down to 3 nursings a day

Week 4 – Get down to 2 nursings a day

Week 5 – Get down to 1 nursing a day (first thing in the morning)

Week 6 – Stop nursing entirely (or hope toddler happens to get distracted one morning, and use as a natural stopping point)

You can stretch this 6 week plan to last as long as you want, and you can also go the other way and condense it down as best you can. In theory, you can use the same approach to wean in only 3 weeks, by doing 2 weeks worth of weaning work each week. For example:

Week 1

Monday - Wednesday – Don't offer, don't refuse

Thursday - Sunday – Get down to 4 nursings a day

Week 2

Monday - Wednesday - Get down to 3 nursings a day

Thursday - Sunday – Get down to 2 nursings a day

Week 3

Monday - Wednesday - Get down to only morning nursing

Thursday - Sunday – Stop nursing entirely

For us, we stuck to the 6 week plan I outlined, but actually spread that last week's plan out over a few weeks -- thus, it took about 8 weeks to fully wean. The approach I've outlined can be modified to fit your needs and preferences, but I'm offering what I did and what worked for us in the pages that follow. Here's how these weeks played out for us...

Week 1 – Don't Offer, Don't Refuse

I started doing the "don't offer, don't refuse" method (which is exactly what it sounds like. For the first week after he was night weaned, I nursed him first thing in the morning (when Mr. Sun came up), and continued to nurse on demand during the day.

Week 2 – Get Down to 4 Nursings by Using Distractions

I nursed him as soon as we woke up, but for the rest of the day, I tried to get us down to 4 set nursing times: (1) first thing in the morning (as already mentioned), (2) right before his nap, (3) when he awoke from his nap, and (4) before we went upstairs for bedtime. In between these 4 sessions, I started distracting him from nursing so that I could sort of delay nursings (and therefore decrease their frequency to a manageable amount of times in the day). I did this without explicitly saying things like "no, we'll do it later," or anything — instead, I literally distracted him. For example, I'd really excitedly point to something and grab him to go look at it, or suddenly get excited about a puzzle or something random.

Full disclosure, this was a a *lot* more of an effort than just nursing when he'd ask, but I was really trying to get us down to a manageable amount of nursing sessions without explicitly making it into a thing. I worried if I communicated what I was doing, he'd comprehend somehow, and resist. (I don't know if that's very rational, but that was my thinking, and it did work for us, so I have no regrets.)

Week 3 – Get Down to 3 Nursings
by Using Distractions

Using the exact same strategy as the previous week, I cut out the nursing right after his nap. It wasn't too hard, because right when he awoke, I brought him a sippy cup of almond milk, and did my super excitable thing to point to distractions and quickly get him out of bed and downstairs. By the end of the week, we were down to three nursings total: (1) first thing in the morning, (2) right before naptime, and (3) before going upstairs for bedtime.

Week 4 – Get Down to 2 Nursings
by Using Distractions

To cut out the nursing session right before naptime, I obviously couldn't use the same strategy as before, since I wouldn't want to rile him up by excitedly pointing to fun distractions right before his intended nap. So instead, I tried the same strategies we used when night weaning: I showed him mouse videos on YouTube, sang lullabies, rocked him and/or patted his butt, and/or hugged him to sleep. It did take a few days during that week, but I think he made the connection that naps, like bedtime, would now not include being nursed to sleep.

So by the end of the week, he was only nursing (1) first thing in the morning, and (2) before we went upstairs for bedtime.

Week 5 – Get Down to Only Nursing
First Thing in the Morning

The next week, I went back to my distracting thing to cut

out the before-bedtime nursing, and managed to get us down to just nursing first thing in the morning.

Weeks 6 and 7 – Talk About What's Coming Next

The next two weeks, we continued to nurse only first thing in the morning, and if he ever got confused about our new lifestyle and asked during the day, I'd very matter-of-factly remind him "we don't do that during the day, silly! we just have dudhu in the morning!"

And then... I also started casually (and frequently) bringing up how soon, we wouldn't have dudhu at all anymore, we'd just drink milk from a cup like a big kid. (I really, really, really feel like he understood.)

So I set a date in my calendar, for right after he hit the 18 month mark, and decided that would be the last morning we'd nurse. The next day, we wouldn't. I marked it like that, as "our last nursing session" (rather than as "don't nurse starting this day") because our last nursing session felt like a special, important thing. It was, after all, like the end of a physical oneness; I'd carried him in my tummy for 9 months, and then nursed him almost 18 months — over two years of my life had included my physically providing him nourishment, safety, protection, and love.

I felt apprehensive, nervous, and even emotional in anticipation of this momentous day. I was sure I'd cry, I was sure it would be a powerful experience, and I just all around put a lot of emotional weight on that upcoming day.

Except a few days before "The Big Day" of our final nursing session, my toddler flipped the script. For the first time ever, as soon as he woke up, rather than asking to nurse, he suddenly scrambled out of bed, and away from me. (He saw something on the floor he wanted to play with.)

I was... I don't even have the words now, months and months later, to explain how baffled, confused, deflated, and relieved I was. I didn't have to stop him from nursing. He just forgot about it and didn't ask. And since my pre-planned final nursing session was just a few days away anyway, I obviously wasn't going to try to start us back up again and then stop him from nursing. It was obviously much better that it happened organically.

Week 8 (and beyond) – Mission Toddler Weaning: Complete

He still occasionally asked, usually first thing in the morning, for dudhu, and I'd just remind him, "Oh! we don't do that anymore, remember? Let's go get food!" and we'd head down. I was also under no delusions that he'd automatically repeat the same behavior the next day... I figured I'd have to reinforce what just happened and explicitly communicate that now we don't nurse anymore at some point in the near future. Which happened.

In fact, for weeks and weeks after, he'd randomly still ask (especially if he saw me getting changed or something), but in those instances, I'd usually make it into a funny/silly thing like "Hey, are you making a joke? We don't do that anymore! You're funny!" and he'd start laughing (why do kids love being called silly?) and then I'd distract him. He'd also occasionally ask if he got a boo-boo, and again, I'd either distract, or offer kisses.

So that's how we managed to accomplish "Toddler Weaning" in 8 weeks, but that same series of steps can really easily be whittled down to just 6 weeks, as outlined at the beginning of this chapter.

Finally, know that even if it takes more (or less) time than you anticipated, it will still work out. Whether you condense the steps I've outlined down into just a few short weeks, or stretch them out over the rest of the year, you will get there.

I know, and you know, that weaning can be hard. But I hope that this book has been helpful in alleviating at least some of the ache, the challenges, and certainly, the confusion, that can come with deciding to wean and making it happen, and that you feel, even slightly more prepared to wean your toddler. And when you do finally, successfully bring your nursing relationship to a close (and you will!), I hope you will feel the warmth that comes with the knowledge that you have done a great job sustaining your nursing relationship this long, and a great job bringing it to a gentle, gradual close.

You've got this.

RESOURCES

More on Breastfeeding and Weaning

I f you're at the point that you've just finished reading this book on toddler weaning, you likely already know everything you might want to know about breastfeeding and/or weaning. That said, maybe you're going to be entering another breastfeeding relationship with another baby soon. If that's the case, I would say there is no downside to learning more about breastfeeding. To that point, I'm sharing some of the resources I found most useful in learning to breastfeed and even about the female body in context of nursing:

1. Joining a good breastfeeding support community (e.g. a support group on Facebook)

2. Talking to friends who also nursed or were currently nursing about our experiences

3. The website of La Leche League (LLL) - The LLL website is an awesome hub of information, and an IRL organization that likely has a chapter near you and free support for BFing moms, including the option to call and chat with a chapter leader if you ever have any questions or need support. (The indexing for their articles/posts has changed, and some of my favorite articles have moved around on their site, but you can search for whatever topics you want

once at either of those sites, and you'll find a wealth of great information).

4. KellyMom.com - I found KellyMom immensely helpful. The website is full of great articles.

5. CafeMom has a post from that compiles a list of the 50 best breastfeeding resources on the web.

6. The book *Boobin' All Day Boobin' All Night: A Gentle Approach to Sleep for Breastfeeding Families* by Meg Nagle

7. Deciding to think of nursing as something I was "going to stick to, not just something I would *try* to do."

I know that for me, my being able to have a great nursing relationship last time around (with my older son), was really just a matter of amazing luck. I was offered the right words of support at the right time. When I learned to breastfeed with my first child, I was lucky to have had those supports, but things could have gone differently. The supports I did have helped arm me against a lot of well-meaning (but ultimately bad) advice that could have really hurt my nursing relationship. So while I was lucky to have had good supports, it would have been helpful to go in consciously prepared. The second time around, I was certainly more knowledgeable and confident, having nursed my first child, but I also found the best resource of all -- the amazing book, *The Womanly Art of Breastfeeding*. After my second child was born, I started reading *The Womanly Art of Breastfeeding* (really, the bible of nursing a baby). And as I read, I keep thinking, I wish I'd had this book when my older son was born (or while I was expecting him). If I'd read this book then, it would have been so very helpful.

If you're heading into nursing another baby -- whether you haven't yet weaned a toddler, or you're newly pregnant, or already nursing a baby, I highly recommend buying this book, and reading it cover to cover. Even as a second time around nursing mom, I found the book informative, validating, and sometimes exactly what I needed.

Finally, and relatedly: If you're not already familiar with how to understand your fertility signs, I highly recommend it. Understanding your own fertility is one of the most empowering and enlightening things you can do, and when you start understanding your body's fertility signals, it can truly help you to better understand your body. Some useful resources:

If you're just starting out, I highly recommend the app Fertility Friend.

Many women swear by the book Taking Charge of your Fertility.

Naturalwomanhood.org has good posts about understanding fertility signs, specifically while breastfeeding.

Wholeparentingfamily.com also has another good post about figuring out fertility postpartum.

It is sincerely my hope that these resources are helpful, and that they help empower you to better understand your body.

And, I hope that this book has been similarly empowering; I hope that the preceding pages have been helpful in making you feel better prepared for your own journey in weaning. I know that everyone's journey to bring their breastfeeding relationship with their child to a close will look different. I know that what has been described in these pages may not work for every mother-child dyad. I also know that for some of the mamas reading this book, how you ultimately succeed (and you will) in weaning might look nothing like the plans I've offered here. But if reading this book has offered you some sense of control over the mostly uncontrollable, and given you a feeling that you at least have some kind of plan, then I am grateful.

I hope, most of all, that this book has helped you to feel seen. Because no matter what it is about weaning that you're finding difficult, you are not alone, and other mothers, now and for millennia before us, have considered some of these feelings.

You've done beautifully, mama.

ACKNOWLEDGEMENTS

I want to offer words of thanks to the friends who offered words of feedback and help in putting together this book: Dr. Natalie Duvall and Dr. Alexandra Murtaugh, thank you for your careful and patient feedback on inclusivity in this work.

I'm also thankful to La Leche League, KellyMom.com, for providing resources that make breastfeeding easier for so many new moms. And it has to be stated, I am so thankful to the book *The Womanly Art of Breastfeeding*, for existing.

Thank you to the people who said the right things at the right times in my own breastfeeding journey with my kids; I'm thankful to the nurses who helped us figure out how to latch, to the old friend who reached out to offer words of support and to encourage me to breastfeed, to my own mother for telling me not to think of breastfeeding as something I would "attempt," but to think of it as something I would stick to, and to my husband David, for encouraging me and us on this journey, and for the moral support as that journey came to an end.

And most of all, thank you to my kids for sharing in this experience with me. I'm thankful for the gift of having nursed my children. (And just as thankful that it's a gift that comes with an expiration date!)

ABOUT THE AUTHOR

Punita C. Rice, Ed.D is a teacher and a mom of two. She is also an education researcher and the founder of ISAASE, an outreach organization aimed at improving student experiences. She writes about student experiences, multicultural education, and equity (selected writing at PunitaRice.com/writing), as well as about motherhood and being intentional about being a happy mom, on her blog, Happy Mom Guide. She is the author of *Toddler Weaning: Deciding to Gradually Wean your Toddler & Making it Happen*, and *South Asian American Experiences in Schools: Brown Voices from the Classroom*.

Punita earned her Doctorate in Education from Johns Hopkins University, where she researched South Asian American experiences, especially in context of teacher cultural proficiency. She then went on to start ISAASE, an outreach organization aimed at improving student experiences in schools. Her book on South Asian American experiences in schools is based on her research.

Punita lives in Maryland with her husband and their two boys. She drinks a lot of coffee.

More works by the author

Punita writes about a variety of topics, including education, multicultural education, South Asian American experiences, and equity. She also writes about motherhood, and being intentional about being a happy mom, on her blog Happy Mom Guide. You can view some of her selected writing at her website, PunitaRice.com.

You can view more books by Punita Rice that are available on Amazon on her Amazon author page.

ENDNOTES

---

[1] And about what it means that many offices offer lactation rooms and time for pumping as a means of being "family friendly," but do not offer flexible hours or paid leave… but I digress.

[2] And both WHO and AAP agree that the first six months of this should be "exclusive" breastfeeding (meaning, the infant receives nothing other than breastmilk for nourishment), since, according to WebMD, "babies who are breastfed exclusively for the first 6 months, without any formula, have fewer ear infections, respiratory illnesses, and bouts of diarrhea."

[3] Perhaps part of why we feel uncomfortable with the prospect of nursing in public (or, even with the idea of people knowing we are nursing our babies past a particular age) is because it is not something we see happening openly. It could be argued that the real solution to this is to work to help normalize it. If we are, in fact, more open about nursing our babies in public, we might be helping make it easier for other moms to do the same. To wit, last year I saw a neighbor of mine sitting outside on a bench in our community, nursing her baby -- publicly, proudly. It was largely the reason why, only a few weeks later, I nursed my younger son in public, without a cover, for the first time (I used the two-shirt method -- top shirt gets pulled up, bottom shirt/nursing tank gets pulled down, baby nurses from between those two, so I was still pretty discreet about it, but it was still a milestone for me in my journey as a nursing mom). As someone once told me, "Every time you nurse in public, you give another mom permission to nurse in public." After all, it's no coincidence that I did it just a week after seeing my neighbor do it; seeing another mom nurse in public helps normalize it, and helps empower us to do the same. Nursing in public gives other moms permission to do so; this can also be true about nursing our toddlers.

[4] As a note about the study: In my opinion, it is plausible that there may be an issue with the generalizability of this data. Most studies don't exam-

ine the experience of moms who are *truly* following all of the principles of ecological breastfeeding, and because moms who do so make up a minority, it is reasonable to imagine that self-reported adherence to ecological breastfeeding is not 100% reliable. All of this to say, I think when we start to see that spike in return to fertility, we are also likely seeing a slight decrease in adherence to the 7 principles of ecological breastfeeding. That said, this is still incredibly helpful information, particularly for moms trying to make sense of their fertility while still nursing.

[5] According to Dr. Sears, "fertility hormones tend to be highest during the sleeping hours," so nursing at night might be critical to continuing to produce the "hormones that suppress ovulation."

[6] One of my dear friends who was trying to night wean her sweet daughter tried to read Nursies When The Sun Shines to her daughter, and it completely backfired: As soon as her daughter heard "nursies" in the book, she wanted to be nursed, and took it upon herself to "help herself" by yanking her mom's shirt down. And that was the end of that. That is to say, your mileage may vary.

Made in the USA
Monee, IL
07 December 2019

18132986R00035